T0107644

Addicted to Pain

Addicted to Pain

Eric Maurice Clark

Order this book online at www.trafford.com
or email orders@trafford.com

© Copyright 2012 Eric Maurice Clark.
Foreward by Bishop Troy Garner

All rights reserved. No part of this publication may be reproduced, stored in a retrieval
system, or transmitted, in any form or by any means, electronic, mechanical, photocopying,
recording, or otherwise, without the written prior permission of the author.

Printed in the United States of America.

ISBN: 978-1-4669-1962-4 (sc)
ISBN: 978-1-4669-1963-1 (e)

Trafford rev. 04/25/2012

 www.trafford.com

North America & international
toll-free: 1 888 232 4444 (USA & Canada)
phone: 250 383 6864 ✦ fax: 812 355 4082

Contents

I Dedicate This Book To

Denise Vaughn "your strength has enabled me
to continue on my journey to my destiny"

Thanks to all my family and friends
for your continual support.

Eric Maurice Clark

MANY ARE THE afflictions of the righteous, but the Lord delivers him out of them all. Psalms 34:19

In the writings of my spiritual son Eric Maurice Clark, he conveys his thoughts according to the young adult experience in today's society. Clark's tolerance to pain, people and the struggle from lost identity is well noted in this second book. Clark once again becomes very iridescent in his writing. What intrigues my interest about this particular book, the author cuts no corners in relating to his point of view and challenges of his time associated with turmoil and lost identity.

When you have an experience such as Clark, I'm sure that the pen can never totally express the tolerance of affliction one after another. However, Clark bravely and candidly expresses his involvement and his compromise with individuals that affected and afflicted his posture as a young man.

I first noticed Clark's strength at his father's celebration of life when there was no unity in his family structure, and Clark was able to deal with the tragedy of death and remain strong and firm in his Christian values.

As I have read this manuscript I wept with sorrow because there was so much information that Clark did not share. Now I can imagine only a God could have brought him through his trials and tribulations. The hope of salvation has been spoken over Clark's life and I know God has a plan and purpose in store for Clark.

As you read this second book of Clark, the question that should plague your interest is: What is the next generation experiencing? Now here's your answer in the writing of Eric Clark.

God bless you Eric M. Clark

This is your finest hour,
Bishop Troy Garner Sr.

Addicted To Pain

AFTER I WROTE my first book "*The Experience (Near To death)*", as I was trying to get back into the regular feel of life, I found myself feeling guilty. I felt guilty after realizing I was holding back my gift that God placed inside of me. I wasn't living in my calling; I was just trying to make things work without fully owning up to what was inside of me.

I truly felt terrible inside after seeing how much my book was impacting the lives of many others. I stated to myself, "Lord I'm sorry for living such a careless life". I felt comfortable with my life just working and partying. I wasn't trying to find my calling at that point in my life anymore. I began to relax in my daily life routine; not doing anything more. I had given up on myself in a way.

I was neglecting all my hidden talent because of past failures. Oh, how I felt guilty knowing that God had spared my life countless times in the past. It seems as though this hasn't received my attention before. How many times has God spared your life? Are you living in your calling? So I ask the question, "Do you have guilt? What are you guilty of?"

Guilt is a powerful tool that can be used very diversely. Guilt can bring conviction to the mind of a person. Guilt: a feeling of responsibility or remorse for some offense, crime, wrong, etc., whether real or imagined. It's our responsibility to understand the consequences of our own actions. Guilt has a way of getting the very best of you when you dwell on the cause of the guilt. I have felt guilty of many things before in the past, and I've also been guilty of things in my past. My guilt has always found a way to get me in order.

While in a conversation with a close friend, my friend privileged me by sharing his touching story. Sometimes it only takes one time that a parent is absent from their child that can cause a change in the direction in the child's life. It's amazing how a child can grow up thinking things were one way, but in actuality, things were another way. My friend shared with me how just recently he came into the knowledge of a horrible encounter that one of his immediate family members was forced to experience.

My friend's sister was being molested by another family member; although, many times we may hear similar stories of such content; I've found out that it's never the same until it hits home. As I listened to the life-touching ordeal, I couldn't help but mentally note the importance of communication amongst brothers and sisters. The pain of hearing this story was kind of unbearable due to the mere fact that my friend is fully grown with his sister still yet in high school.

My friend's sister was being inappropriately touched and fondled by her own cousin. She told him that this was happening on a regular basis. ("What a hard piece of knowledge to hear at such an awkward time") "Guilt" is what my friend stressed the most; he had guilt because he just couldn't understand how he allowed that to happen;

he informed me that he was left in charge to watch over his siblings as his mother was dealing with other issues. I encouraged him and told him it wasn't his fault.

The only way to recover from this guilt that now lives in his heart is through the power of "forgiving". Sometimes it only takes "you" to forgive yourself to heal the people in your inner circles. The power of guilt is a powerful weapon that promotes much needed change.

So many times we ask the question "Why". Why must I bear this pain? Why don't I have what I want? Why am I treated so badly? Why do I feel unappreciated? Why? We ask those questions, but can we really handle the truth?

Everyone has experienced pain one way or another in their lives. Sometimes we even feel that we experience some pain continually. Pain; of being, in bad relationships, pain of being mistreated, pain of rejection, physical pain, mental pain; "pain", whatever it may be.

Some pain indicates it's time to pay attention; on the other hand, pain warns our body as well as our mind of potential danger. Danger should always be taken into consideration. Danger is a place or placement where safety cannot be found.

Whenever you reach the point of pain, realize that either it's time to pay attention or danger is lurking somewhere. Sometimes, we began to not take heed to pain. Pain can be used as a warning that can help change the destination that's awaiting you. Rather emotional or physical pain, it helps warn you of issues that maybe occurring—don't allow your issues to control you.

One unbearable pain I have experienced countless of times is emotional pain due to relationship problems. I have found myself in an emotional wreck time and time again. I now realize that my desires of wanting nothing more than happiness in a relationship were causing me to abort my future. You must first be happy with who you are before you can be happy in a relationship with someone else. You have to first love yourself in order to love someone else. If you don't truly love yourself it will hinder you from allowing someone else to love you. It's almost impossible for a person to love you if you don't truly love yourself. Loving yourself sincerely will keep you rooted and grounded so that you don't settle for the unnecessary.

Sometimes, due to stages in our past, we find ourselves immune to the routine system that's utilized on a regular basis in our lives. We build a tolerance for what we continuously allow ourselves to face.

Routine that's usually followed: consistency of past failures, remaining in hazardous environments, staying in unhealthy relationships, lack of educating rebellions, reframing from relief of poor relationship skills, sincerely attacking peace, sincerely giving up bad habits, "etc".

Consistency of past failures is an unsuccessful tactic. Failures can be used as a map. In using the failure map you will find the directions to failure. With that in mind, don't take the same route that is shown on the failure map. Think of it as an old outdated map of roads which doesn't exist anymore. An outdated map is pretty much useless.

Antiques are items that are old or old fashion. The worth of an antique is the value in which the person of interest is willing to accept. Some antiques are still held at its original worth as some are worth more. Consider your past as an antique—what is the value of your past? That question is analyzed by your progress, maturity and determination. Your past processes important tools that incorporate the completeness of your true existence. You have the option of making the worth of your past more valuable by taking heed of your past. Don't allow your past to be worthless. One of the ways you can allow your past to be worthless is giving up. When you give up, you forfeit the game, don't forfeit your life.

Your life has a purpose given by God. Sometimes we put our purpose on hold due to lack of completion. Completing a task is simply showing progress and accomplishment. God has so much in store for us. We lack because of hesitation to tap into the source of supplements. Hesitation is a form of addiction. Initially, hesitation is basically an option; you are the only person who can allow yourself to hesitate. Hesitation can block your future if you allow it to. With knowledge you shouldn't hesitate that which are facts. There's no need to hesitate trusting in God, He won't fail you.

Growth is very vital to accomplishing goals, success and procession of stable ownership. Growth will indicate progress. I had to realize that I wasn't going to ever amount to more than my past if I never learned how to grow pass my past. Growth reveals maturity because you can't grow if you don't mature. **Proverbs 16:3,** "*Commit thy works unto the Lord, and thy thoughts shall be established*". If we commit our works to the Lord our thoughts shall establish, meaning, the beginning of our works are started by first committing. Committing to change is a step of maturity. You have to change mentally in order to see a change physically.

There are many addictions in life. The first step to recovery of any addiction is first acknowledging there is a created habit. Addictions are created habits. What are some of your created habits? The routine of doing the same thing over and over is an addiction. The Lord wants our minds, but there's No Way God can fully use us when we're not willing to let go of our bad habits. An addiction will break the very foundation of self will. Sometimes in your self will you'll find yourself not even being in control due to an addiction ("created habit"). When creating a habit you should first identify with the principal of the habit. In the creation of new habits, when you truly learn the identity of the habit, you can then choose if it's what's you're willing to deal with.

Habits are things that you allow to exist. What is constantly existing in your life that's causing you pain? ("Thank you Jesus"). Is your pain causing you major problems in your life? Where is the root to your pain? Why must this pain hurt so badly?

The Lord has a way of getting our attention. The Lord uses pain to get our attention and to warn us. How long must a warning warn you before you take heed? Taking heed proves that there is an issue. Building a strategy that will effectively remove you from a mental malfunction. Now let's view some of the starting points and participation of being addicted to pain.

Recognizing the root
of bad Addictions

BAD ADDICTIONS FIRST start as thoughts and then lead into bad addictions. If you dwell on negative thoughts, they will eventually become negative actions. Recognizing the root of a bad addiction is recognizing the principal of the addiction. If the principal of the addiction is negative, then the addiction is bad. For example, the principal of studying is to learn; if you don't study you won't learn; since the principal of studying is to learn, studying is considered a positive habit. Whatever may be the reason why you open the option of entertaining the created habit is the root of the addiction.

First Timothy 6:10, "For the love of money is the root of all evil: which while some coveted after, they have erred from the faith, and pierced themselves through with many sorrows." Here is a prime example of the root of bad addictions that will lead you into pain. For the love of money is the root of all evil. Money is a medium that can be exchanged for goods and services and is used as a measure of their values on the market.

Bad addictions are finding exchanges for self gratification; they put your destiny in danger. Like the bible states, the root of all evil is the love of money, meaning whatever can be exchanged for goods and services is your first priority. Whenever your first priority is obtaining goods and services as a misused habit, it's evil. First Timothy 6:9 *"But those who desire to be rich fall into temptation, into a snare, into many senseless and harmful desires that plunge people into ruin and destruction."* Your self-gratification shouldn't be a priority of gold, silver, self pleasure, control, fame, self worshiping, mischievous leadership, etc. If indeed your first priority is such of what was listed, it's a bad addiction.

Your first priorities should always be what it takes to fulfill God's plans for your life. The root of bad addictions is usually what first brought the bad, created habit. Whatever started your desire of wanting that which is bad for you is the root of your bad addiction. For the love of whatever it is, determines whether it's a bad addiction. You pierce yourself with the love of a self desire that puts the essence of "you" on the line. The foundation of a habit determines the level that it has control over you.

I remember wanting a best friend badly, someone I can be close to. I would literally try to befriend everyone. As I seen other people's friendships, I constantly asked myself, "Why don't I have a best friend?" I thought that it was so very cool to have a best friend from childhood. I noticed a lot of best friends were best friends since childhood. So many times I cried mentally due to the misunderstanding I had towards friendships. I honestly just wanted a close friendship type relationship with another person. A lot of the people in my life at that time I called friend had a lot of other alternative motives. I would find myself being someone who I wasn't to fit in so I could have the title friend. Many times we find ourselves compromising our identity to please others. Compromising is a huge revolving door that some people find themselves in and out of, not going anywhere. Trapped in the entrance but never entering.

There was a time when just about all of my peers were smoking marijuana. It seemed like those were the ones who had all the girls and the most adventurous times. I tried smoking to try to fit in, and found myself in the hospital shortly after doing so. I was scared for my life, I felt like I was having a heart attack, my heart felt like it was racing out of my chest. I was so embarrassed; my mother had called my Grandfather to come to the hospital and pray for me. I mentally said to myself, "if I made it out of this, I wouldn't never smoke that stuff again." At the time I felt like I meant it. I used to be so embarrassed of this story, because I felt like, who goes to the hospital for smoking marijuana?

About a year later I was trying to hang out with a popular crowd, but once again, they smoked marijuana. I would hang out with the crowd and try my best to be cool so I could fit in. When they would smoke and my turn would come to smoke, I remember I would act like I was inhaling but in all actuality, I was only blowing the smoke back out my mouth. Sometimes, as I saw them beginning the preparation for smoking marijuana, I would come up with an excuse to leave. The day came that I couldn't fake my inhaling any longer, I had the choice to leave or really inhale. (They had caught on to me not inhaling) So I inhaled the marijuana around the second time the marijuana came my way and I was already feeling the way I felt the last time. Finally, when the marijuana was all smoked up, I was one of the first to head out the door to go home. I remember I went home and I got straight in the bed to see if I could sleep off the way I was feeling. I rocked from side to side trying to ease my troubled mind and body. I shortly found myself finding my dad and calling 911. In my mind I was thinking, here we go again, I have broken a promise to myself trying to be down. I was being someone I wasn't to try to fit in.

The desire of having a close friend resulted in neglecting me to please others. I have built a cage around the inner me and everything that was in the open wasn't me. I would be in church with some and out partying with others. By this action I found myself in chaos in both avenues of friendship that I was choosing. Sometimes your desires will override your priorities.

I found myself being misused, unappreciated, taken advantage of, and a lot of other devious actions. Just because of the desire to have a best friend, I desired an illusion of the principal. Proverbs 27:6, "*Faithful are the wounds of a friend; but the kisses of an enemy are deceitful.*" In this Scripture we find that true friends will be honest even when it hurts; untrue friends are deceitful.

Through this experience, I found out that I had to examine the people who were in my life kissing me, but yet deceitful. It hurts to befriend someone and as a rebate you get hurt. I was hurting myself because of a desire. This desire may be small to some but it's yet huge to others; having a best friend. The bigger picture of the matter People will treat you the way you allow them to treat you. If you don't like it, change the power you allow them to have over you.

So, I found this to be an addiction, wanting a best friend; which was a created habit that I allowed to cause me pain. What an addiction to have, leading you into isolation. Yes I isolated myself because of my own self desires of wanting a best friend. It's amazing how I didn't want to share this struggle with no one; I was even more scared of never finding the friendship I was in search of. I created a habit of wanting friends because I allowed myself to be affected by my inner insecurities. Friendships are only what you make of them, even if you never find someone to call friend, the best friend you could ever have is you. Learn how to love you more than enough.

It's amazing how a desire can turn into an addiction, which can lead into pain. As I think about it now, what in the world was I thinking about at the time? Sometimes your desires will blind you to the obvious. It should have been obvious that I was in an addiction because I was compromising my identity for such a poor reason.

The Lord has so much love for us that he continuously befriends us even when we don't make him our first priority. The Lord will withhold some things for our protection. The Lord is a friend to the friendless. Proverbs 18:24, "A man that hath friends must shew himself friendly: and there is a friend that sticketh closer than a brother." So in other words, I had friends but I was failing to show myself friendly to the ones that were true to me. I'm finding out that a lot of people who are troubled over friendship issues (referring to lack of friends), have true friends, but blind themselves from them.

Never lie to obtain friendship; you'll find when you gain that friendship, it's already contaminated.

So the Lord revealed these things to me about this addiction. First, when you find yourself circling over friendships, look to God for that inner peace and comfort that you may be searching for. An addiction such as this is something very hard to face but is yet painful to deal with. It's hard to deal with the feeling of being a loner. Remember that if you have to sacrifice your identity for a selfish desire, it's not worth it.

I found out through this experience that this painful addiction is also one of the best kept secrets among people. I have learned many people don't want to openly deal with their friendship dilemmas, it's not an easy subject to openly discuss, but yet very important and serious.

The pain that's experienced in this addiction is a recycled pain, because the person doesn't break the habit. As well as it is an emotional pain, it can turn into physical pain. Sometimes what bothers us emotionally, we will let it lead into physical pain. When we dwell on this pain mentally, we began to physically feel pain.

Gather the reasoning of why friendship is such a priority; when you gather the answers to this question, began to place things in their proper place. Encouraging yourself plays a major role in overcoming such an addiction. You have to speak positive to yourself to remove any negativity that may be speaking on your behalf. You are just as important as your neighbor; you must realize and believe this.

Now I have shed light on such an addiction that to some may just be normal. Think about this addiction ("created habit")!! Are you making the desire of friendship a number one priority in your life?

Rejection

FEELING "UNWANTED" IS a feeling that a majority of people don't want to feel. Feeling unwanted is a horrible feeling. When you feel unwanted by others, sometimes you make yourself feel unwanted to you. Not wanting to do anything, go anywhere, even eating food is a result of your allowing this rejection feeling to occupy your life. Rejection is a feeling of being unwanted.

In the feeling of rejection some often feel as though their efforts just aren't good enough. This is a placement that we have the control of placing our own minds in. You have to remember as the bible says in John 15:18, *"If the world hates you, know that it has hated me before it hated you";* which means that before we were born, there was rejection already existing. Jesus was rejected by his own people; so many times we may be rejected by the people in our own circles. Sometimes you may feel as if those are the only ones who reject you. A lot of times we have the fear of rejection before we even get rejected.

For you to feel the pain of rejection from another person, you must first want to be where that person is; which starts at a mental state. The first acknowledgment of this pain starts mentally, because you must first allow it to affect your mind. When it affects your mind, it then starts to venture out physically. It begins to turn into a routine of satisfaction; you then want their company mentally as well as physically.

The pain of rejection turns into an addiction when you continually place your mind and space in the presence of individuals that don't want you around. Then you will find yourself constantly feeling this pain of rejection; which you have created a habit of desiring. This pain will continue to recycle if you continue to dwell in this undesirable situation (in the presence of someone who does not want you there). Continuing in this situation turns into a circle with no end to it. Now you are addicted and don't even realize that it was you who caused such repeated pain. Addicted to pain, so to speak, is now manifesting.

The fear of rejection will hold you back from obtaining goals, dreams, success and so many other things. The fear of rejection comes from creating a habit of prejudging the outcome of things. The fear of rejection is also an addiction which is a created habit that you have actively given attention to. The fear of rejection is a state of mind.

The Rejection Story

THERE WAS A man who lived in the south by himself; all he ever wanted was to feel appreciated. He was born in the city, but due to fear of rejection, he moved to the South to isolate himself from the rest of society. He was the only child, his parents died when he was at the age of 18. His parents were the only people that he felt loved by.

In his childhood he was wrapped in the protection of his parents; he never had friends. His parents kept him in home school throughout his grammar and high school life. He never got a chance to mingle with others in his age group. Everywhere he went, his parents took him, everything he had, his parents supplied; his parents were wealthy.

His parent raised him this way to try to protect him from ever being mentally damaged by other people. They wanted only the best for him. His parents kept him away from the rest of his peers; they wanted to avoid him from experiencing what they experienced in their past. They were bitter because of being rejected in the past.

When his parents died they left him all of their riches because he was their only heir. Life really took a toll on him when his parents died. He never knew how to survive on his own due to being wrapped under the protection of his parents. He never knew what it felt like to have friends; Because of such an isolated childhood, he was scared of the outside society.

He moved to the South after the death of his parents because the only life that he knew was that of an isolated life. He had built a fear of the outside world since he was caged inside the boundaries of his parents. His parent's death had moved him into a deeper isolation from society. His parents were cremated without having a celebration ceremony of their lives. After the death of his parents, he found himself an emotional wreck, as the only people he knew were now gone.

Deep inside he was terrified of being rejected by the rest of society, this was a created habit due to his isolation. He found himself addicted to isolation which caused him pain both mentally and physically. There in the South he had no neighbors, it was just he alone. He had his groceries, personal hygiene items and everything else delivered to him. He never went out because of this fear of rejection he had formed within his mind.

He feared not being accepted; therefore he neglected all of his hidden talent. His intelligence was far advanced than the average person; the man was educated. He never went to college because he was scared of people; so he neglected even online college courses.

Due to his addiction of isolation, mentally he caused self-inflicted pain. The many years of this routine of isolation caused him to never become anything in life. So all his life he feared rejection because of the environment that his parents surrounded him in.

To make a long story short, he passed at the age of 19; never accomplished any goals, dreams, "etc". This story proves how isolation can move a person into rejection causing a created habit that will cause you to abort everything that's within you. He lived one year after the death of his parents; cutting his life short due to a created habit of isolation.

If you never venture beyond four walls, you will never gain access to your future. The fear of rejection can lead you into self bondage. Come to find out that every potential that this young man had never came to pass because of his fear of rejection. Don't allow your past to block your future. Just because you never been to the Bahamas doesn't mean you can't go.

Although your past may have not been what you wanted it to be, doesn't mean you have to continue living in the past. You will find yourself just like the young man in the story, holding back from ever amounting to anything more than his past. In this story the young man's parents created an isolated environment for him because of their past. A lot of time people treat other people the way they feel they were treated, which causes a pattern for redundant behavior. Just because you may have went through some sort of rejection doesn't mean you have to involve other people in your world. If his parents had allowed him the chance to find his own identity, he would not have given up on life.

When you feel like giving up, that's the best time to get back down on your knees and cry out to the Lord. Sometimes the Lord scrambles things around in your life to get your attention. Some bridges need to be destroyed; you don't want dangerous structured bridges in your life. By being privileged to cross over should be enough motivation to destroy the bridge to protect others. Danger is the fear of rejection; lose all ties so you can live out the very essence of your destiny. Allow your past to be your past, move forward toward your purpose.

Don't continue to live in your past and be bound by it. There is so much more to life than to live in rejection. This young man was very wealthy, but his wealth didn't save his mind from the fear of rejection. Not only was his life cut short, he also cut short his destiny; not even having children to carry out his legacy.

The fear of rejection is a state of mind; the fear of rejection starts mentally. You have every right to pursue every dream; don't allow someone to influence your thoughts so that you create a habit of living in the fear of rejection. If you hear yes all the time, you wouldn't know what it takes to work for a yes. There is power in the word no; you need to examine why you received a no. Isolation is a form of self-pity, keeping the inner you from attacking your purpose.

Stop punishing yourself because of rejection by others. Here are some scriptures that you can use very diversely: Romans 12:19, *"Beloved, never avenge yourselves, but leave it to the wrath of God, for it is written, vengeance is mine, I will repay, says the Lord."* Just because someone may treat you wrong, don't punish yourself, for that is an action of vengeance; God says "I will repay, vengeance is mine". The young man in the story killed himself as a move of forfeiture as he no longer wanted to deal with his emotionally driven pain.

Learn to love yourself even if you never feel the type of love that you want from others. Understand that you're smart, intelligent and beautiful enough to make it to your own promise land that God has promised you.

No Other God

Exodus 20:1-26, *"And God spoke all these words, saying, I am the Lord your God, who brought you out of the land of Egypt, out of the house of slavery. "You shall have no other gods before me. You shall not make for yourself a carved image, or any likeness of anything that is in heaven above, or that is in the earth beneath, or that is in the water under the earth. You shall not bow down to them or serve them, for I the Lord your God am a jealous God, visiting the iniquity of the fathers on the children to the third and the fourth generation of those who hate me . . . "*

H ERE GOD IS speaking to the children of Egypt, he's telling them to have no other God before him. When you do a psychological analysis on the things that you want, then find out the pain is relevant to the wants of your desires; use this scripture passage in Exodus as a flashlight. I don't care what it is, it may be: friendships, relationships, material things, etc., if you don't put it before God, you're going to have problems.

I speak very carefully on material things, because you will find out indeed that material things will cause you pain. Making material things a first priority is a created habit; it started somewhere. God wants your attention, he doesn't require that much of you; your attention, is one that he requires. If you don't pay attention to the road while you're driving, you will have an accident shortly thereafter.

Material things can become an addiction, causing you to neglect true principles. **Luke 10:27,** *"And he answered, you shall love the Lord your God with all your heart and with all your soul and with all your strength and with all your mind, and your neighbor as yourself."* Here in this passage you don't see love your house and then God, love your wife and then God, love God after you find employment or etc. The bible is saying, love God with all your heart and with all your soul and so on.

I find a lot of time we as a people base our love for God on destinations meaning, whatever it is we're in search for controls our levels of love toward God. Don't base your love for God as a destination, meaning when you get your desires, then you start loving God. God doesn't require a destination love, God requires a Journey love. Love God and keep his commandments. The Bible states, seek ye first the kingdom of God and all his righteousness, then all the other things shall be added. That inner peace you're in search of is within God. We have to learn to search the kingdom of God more. Applying other Gods in your life look like this: making excuses to God, giving more attention to material things rather than God, praising other people for your accomplishments, judging your love, etc. It's easy to slip up and find yourself in this boat by falling under the spell of material things. Material things are wonderful, but never love them more than God. This is the reason why sometimes we find ourselves in an emotional wreck with our emotions because we have spent more time trying to accomplish our goals without God.

Coming Into Wisdom

WISDOM IS KNOWLEDGE from God; understanding comes from God. **Proverbs 15:2,** *"the tongue of the wise useth knowledge aright: but the mouth of fools poureth out foolishness."* To get an understanding, you must seek God. Your tongue renders knowledge when you speak the word of God. A fool will do nothing more than pour out foolishness. Wise is the man who trusts in the Lord, for his ways are guided by God.

You will find things out of place when you lean not unto the understanding of God. Lean not to your own understanding, but in all thy ways acknowledge God and he will direct thy path. **Proverbs 3:7,** *"Be not wise in thine own eyes: fear the Lord, and depart from evil."* Don't try to make it without the Lord; it won't work. If we travel with our own eyes, we travel carnal minded; spiritually traveling, we will depart from evil because we fear the Lord.

The Lord will place certain obstacles in our path because he's trying to inform you that you're on the wrong path. Pain is one of the obstacles that He uses to warn you that you're traveling in the wrong direction. Learning how to take pit stops along the road, helps you stay on the right path. In the pit stops, you'll find: prayer, fasting, worshipping, praising, the word of God and so much more. Don't forget your pit stop locations are whenever you hear the Lord's voice; you may hear: I need some me time, worship me for who I am, I have a word for you, I have more work for you, you're getting too comfortable; God speaks to help us along the way to make sure we make it to our final destination, "heaven".

God wants to give you the wisdom to surpass all evil, you have to be willing to accept. You don't have to be bound or held in bondage by the irregular emotional pains this world has to offer. If you want to be free from you emotional pain, you should not dwell on the issues and simply let it go. It sounds more easily said than done, determination plays a major role in letting go of bad habits. Wisdom is worldly intangible, it must come from God. Knowledge can only inform you of a matter, but wisdom will protect you.

I Want a Spouse

WANTING SOMEONE SPECIAL that you can call your own intimately is one of the largest requests from the majority of humans. "Everybody seems to want somebody". You have to search until you just couldn't search any longer. "I have been so hurt in the past" is one the most recited phrases that one had heard. A lot of people feel the fear of never finding a perfect mate; that's one of the problems; no one is going to be perfect. Love "true covers a multitude of faults.

Many people go into relationships in the mindset of the other person being perfect, allowing this to rule the relationship. You shouldn't look for your mate to be perfect due to the fact that nobody is perfect. Many people seem to go through breakup after breakup, but never truly understanding the reason why. So many times people experience the same thing in every relationship. Have you ever wondered why? Is it your fault? Why can't I find my soul mate?

Hereto is another created habit that must be broken to succeed over past failures in relationships. Nobody wants to be at fault, but somebody has to be at fault. When you find yourself at the end of another relationship, you should always analyze the relationship to find out what was the problem. Problems relationships face are: cheating, not understanding, insecurities, lack of time, lack of space, wrong interests, rebellions, finance and so many other things. You must first find the root of every situation that could be causing a repeat of failed relationships.

I remember very vividly the discussions me and my father had about this client. My dad said he must have had some type of scheme up his sleeves; it is just remarkably ridiculous to get married four times within five years. I analyzed this for myself and I find that it is not the women in his case but it's him. Four different times, four different women, you must stop and look yourself in the mirror and ask yourself what am I doing wrong? What created habit do I have that's causing many failures? I remember even hearing him state on numerous occasions, "this is the right one now".

Some people don't have such a blunted story as this, but being in and out of relationships is very relevant. I write about this because time and time I've experienced friends as well as family in and out of relationships; wanting nothing more than happiness, but never finding that happiness. Here we are my friend, an addition that was once formed either out of insecurities, infidelity or anything on the subject.

So many people find not only the fear of rejection to people, but they also find the pain of redundant behavior in such matters. It is very painful to feel that you can't find your soul mate. Sometimes your desires for a mate will cause you to detour the right path. Whenever you go into a relationship due to insecurities you will find your insecurities ruling the relationship. The root of this created habit is not just a year ago but it is consistent. Whatever the consistency is, cut it loose; if you don't, you will always find yourself in an allusion of a relationship.

If you continue to blame others for the consistency of failed relationships, you will never overcome this lifestyle. There is something that you were doing wrong but might not realize it. **1 John 1:9,** *"If we confess our sins, he is faithful and just to forgive us our sins and to cleanse us from all unrighteousness."* The Bible states, if you confess your wrong doing, he will cleanse you from all unrighteousness; you first must confess. The Lord is faithful to give you the desires of your heart, but you must first confess your own wickedness. Being bold and not understanding is wickedness. The Bible says, "When pride cometh, then cometh shame", your self-pride will destroy you.

In order to have a successful relationship, you must first put away pride. That client that I gave reference to had a bowl of pride that was killing his love life. Come first into the knowledge of relationships then apply that knowledge accordingly. You can do it, I believe there is somebody for everybody; you just have to submit yourself unto the will of God. For this cycle is very painful, but remember it's a created habit that must be broken.

Insecurities

I'M A FIRM believer that insecurities are mental stumbling blocks. Other people can't see your insecurities until you reveal them. Revealing your insecurities look something like this: your facial expressions, your vibes, your attitude, isolation and countless other expressions. Are you revealing your insecurities?

Insecurities are lacking confidence, pretty much self doubting. The reason why many have lack of confidence is due to past rejection or fear of present rejection. To lack confidence, you have to not believe in yourself; this too has an initial starting point. Lack of confidence will hold you back from exploring your potential options. Insecurities, is as a thief; I truly believe that insecurities will rob you from your future. Insecurities also are an excuse to some; not trying or trying to give up what has already been stated. Insecurities are a form of worthless baggage.

Have you ever thought about where your insecurities came from? Insecurities will make you feel awkward. Feeling awkward is a feeling of being defenseless to certain situations. It all starts from your confidence level being attacked. This is a created habit that started at one point in time.

Ring, ring, ring, Jonathan heard as he sat by his telephone at home. This was yet another distraction to go along with his already stressful day since he had made it home. Jonathan didn't want to speak to no one else for the remainder of the day; he was just too tired to deal with anybody else for the day. Jonathan was a telemarketer that made phone calls throughout his whole work day on a regular basis. This was the best job he could find where he would deal with limited coworkers, yet away from public customers. He would rather hear the dial tone than being disrespected face-to-face by customers.

Such a poor excuse, Jonathan thought in his mind, as he sat there by his ringing telephone. I'm sitting here frustrated because of my job. How stressful my job is, but my insecurities are keeping me in this bondage. I'm too scared to live out my potentials that I am living beneath my privileges.

Now the moral of the story is, Jonathan's insecurities are contradicting.

It may be small, but what is keeping you from your potential? What's holding you back? Jonathan was scared of commuting with others in the public, though it may seem small, this is one of his insecurities. Insecurities will rob you of your future.

What people think of you shouldn't make you degrade yourself. Some people will do their very best to try to derail you. Some people only want to see you fail and never succeed. People will lie on you because they have spied on you and they're jealous of you. When a person is jealous of another person, confrontations are normally involved. **James 3:14-16,** *"But if you have bitter jealousy and* *selfish ambition in your hearts, do not boast and be false to the truth. This is not the wisdom that comes down from above, but is earthly, unspiritual, demonic. For where jealousy and selfish ambition exist, there will be disorder and every vile practice.* " The Bible warns us of jealousy and selfish ambition, don't try to change a person with a jealous heart; God has to deal with that person

There are many forms of jealousy that can cause an envious spirit within a person's heart. Jealousy can be found just about anywhere; church, home, family, workplace, "etc". Along with places which jealousy can be found, there are material things as well where jealousy sets up camp round about; houses, cars, Ipad's, finer cloths, furniture and so many other material things.

Be careful of the things that you make your heart desire after, for some of those very things may cause you to avoid those other things which are important. Sometimes we take those things which are important and list them in our unimportant self priority category. Jealousy reigns around what we place as desirable, finding all kinds of conniving ways to conceive that which we envy for. Being envious is a trick of the enemy to try to reroute you, directing you away from that which is purposed for you.

Strategy

Proverbs 5:23, *"He shall die without instruction; and in the greatness of his folly he shall go astray."* Here's a great word of wisdom shedding light on the destination of one who strays away from instruction. Instruction leads you into the path for that which is concerning you. Understanding the importance of instruction is what combines knowledge and wisdom. That which is foolish maybe foolish, knowingly or unknowingly, sometimes we become foolish because of the fear of either insecurities or rejections.

Whatever pains you may be experiencing, knowing where it comes from is the first step of recovering. Recovering from lustful and unimportant created habits can seem impossible at times, due to the length and how far pushed into the habit you are. Breaking away from unnecessary situations is the determination that must be planted inside your thoughts in order to accomplish that which has defeated you in the past. Your past don't owe you an apology, you owe your present your undivided attention to conquer your future. Leaving out lustful desires will lead you into the trustful promises of God. **Titus 1:2,** *"In hope of eternal life, which God, that cannot lie, promised before the world began."* Here you see God has made promises unto us before the world began, it's up to us to walk into those promises.

Raphael's Concept

RAPHAEL WAS BORN and raised in a little town in Mississippi called Sumrall, about 19 miles from Hattiesburg. He was a retired educator who lived in an old wooden house. So much he enjoyed doing with his dog (Eleanor Rigby) which he had since she was born. Eleanor's parents were Raphael's Grandparent's pets who added so much spice to their lives since they were up in age. To this day Raphael don't have a clue how long his grandparents had the dogs, for as long as he could remember they were always there.

Radcliff was an old grammar school buddy of Raphael who still lived in the town of Sumrall. Radcliff lived by himself in a five bedroom house, not too far from his parent's 40 acres of land. Often people asked him about selling the land, but he didn't want to sell it. The land held sentimental value rooted in his heart. The house that he was born in was there on that land. Nobody ever understood why he didn't want to live there himself, but I guess some people just are personalized when it comes to their desires.

Radcliff came over Raphael's house every Friday early evening around 4:00 pm to conversant and prepare to watch the sunset. Watching the sunset on Fridays stood as a refreshing mental clearance to rest yet another week for the both of them. For almost 20 years, this is what the both of them did weekly. This was something they looked forward to every week.

Raphael's dog "Eleanor Rigby" would come out on the porch routinely every Friday to bathe in their presence; Eleanor must have liked to watch the sunset as well. She had been diagnosed with a case of doggy depression, and the only person who seems to know her problem was Raphael. **("Sometimes the only person who knows your heartaches is you".)** Eleanor dealt with a lot of physical and emotional pain.

Every time Radcliff would come over Raphael's house, his dog would come outside and come to a routine spot. Eleanor would always moan as if he was in a lot of pain. Radcliff worried quite a bit about the moaning of Eleanor. He couldn't understand why. This was one thing he never asked Raphael about, he didn't know how to address it to Raphael. **("Some people are prejudice about other people's opinions".)**

Eventually, one day when Radcliff came over, Eleanor came outside and moaned yet again and stated these words to Raphael ("I've been meaning to ask you this, why is it that every time I come over, Eleanor comes out to the same spot and moan"). Oh don't worry about her, she's just sitting on a nail, Raphael replied. "Why won't you just remove the nail" he asked? There's no need my friend because when she eventually gets tired of feeling the pain, she won't keep coming back to the same spot, was the statement Raphael made.

Whatever it is you may be feeling when you've truly endured enough, you will move from that pain. Pain is a location, if you don't like the pain, change your location.

Changing
Your Location

THOUGH IT IS **a gift, our words have the power to destroy and the power to build up (Proverbs 12:6).** Even though sometimes we may feel like things aren't going to change, we have to watch what we say.

You can change your location by simply speaking it out of your mouth, you have the power. The devil tries fooling us by association (having people to discourage us), don't be hindered by people. God has a plan for your life, always remember that.

Your location speaks silently about you. Trying to change people is sometimes an impossible task, in other words, change yourself; people will see the change in you and want the change for themselves. Whatever location you may be in, understand and study it to make sure it's your location. Being in the wrong location can kill you, your vision, your happiness, your dreams, your spirit, your destiny. Your location is 99% evidence of where you've been. Where have you been? Where are you going?

"Go to the ant, you sluggard! Consider her ways and be wise" (Proverbs 6:6). Get up! Go consider the ways of the wise, determined in your mind to have a change of location. You can't be lazy about change. Sometimes it's your location that causes you to forfeit your happiness. Changing your past determinations can promote you and cause past pain to cease. One way to change your location is resetting your boundaries. What you allow in your life is what you basically mentally state, "I'm willing to put up with". If you allow insecurities to determine your happiness, you'll allow yourself to put up with whatever your insecurities are.

Sometimes you have to make up in your mind that you are not crying over the same thing anymore, rise above "things" and live your life. The inner peace that you may be looking for just may be in your decision of changing things that are out of place in your life. If you're comfortable with your surroundings, change your location mentally as well as physically.

Conclusion

ADDICTED TO PAIN is a figure of speech which revolves around your decision to make a change in the areas that is begging for new placement. You have the power to relocate yourself and make the changes that are necessary, destroying bad created habits. Understand that you must find the root of the bad created habit in order to destroy the habit. Don't allow yourself to fall short due to the lack of determination. People only have the control that you allow them to have over you.

Gain control of your life to overcome whatever it may be constantly reoccurring in your life. God don't throw your prayers away, they're stored up for rainy days . . . Things are going to get better. One of the biggest mistakes you can make is *Giving up*. Place your issues in the hands of the Lord and rest on his promises.

Remember, what you do in your present effects your future; don't get caught up in your insecurities, they will hinder you from your future. Live and be grateful that you're alive even after all that you have been through. Build your own strategy that will lead you closer to God. God is still there waiting on you to acknowledge him. Lustful desires can kill you in the long run; kill your lustful desires with the word of God. Sometimes, you don't always have the control over what comes in your mind. What you do have control over is whether it stays there. For a lustful thought to come into your mind may not be something you can always control. If you keep it in your mind and possibly desire to act upon it, then it becomes wrong.

Your created habits shouldn't be causing you damnation. If they are, you need to kill the habit before it kills you. Being motivated will keep you striving for the changes that are the most important. The devil wants you to believe that things will forever remain the same, and that is a trick; things will get better if you trust in Jesus.

Remember, you don't have to live in unnecessary pain if you only move from that redundant spot. You have the power through Jesus Christ. Follow the voice of Jesus always. No matter how things may look, when you obey the voice of God somebody, somewhere is being blessed by your obedience. Be obedient to the voice of God and come out of that which you're not supposed to be in.

You have a right to love yourself enough to not allow your past to rob you from your future. Don't give up because of your past failures; motivation comes from past failures. Encouraging yourself can deliver you from isolation. It's time to tell your hurt of your past "R.I.P". You can heal yourself by simply "Letting Go". Let go and let God.

421
STUDIOS
WWW.421STUDIOS.NET

THE EXPERIENCE
(NEAR TO DEATH)

ERIC MAURICE CLARK

FOREWARD BY BISHOP MICHAEL D. WILSON